Anti-Black Racism
In
Latin America

Salvatore D. Casco

Published By: Tamika INK

Library of Congress Cataloging-in-Publication Data has been applied for

ISBN: 9798326599711

PRINTED IN THE UNITED STATES OF AMERICA

Acknowledgments

would like to dedicate this book to all my relatives and friends. I would like for this book to create awareness of what takes place in Latin America and people's attitudes toward racism in that region. I have seen the effects of systemic racism and racial injustices against black people in the United States; therefore, it made me want to see the effects of systemic racism against people of African descent in Latin America.

As a Hispanic-American, I feel that it is important for me to understand how systemic racism works in the region where my family is from and what should be done to combat this. After seeing the Black Lives Matter protests in 2020, I wanted to see how entrenched anti-black racism is in Latin American countries. Social justice is an important issue, and we should acknowledge that it is a major issue in Latin America.

Table of Contents

Introduction

In Latin America, there is anti-black racism. Many people may mistakenly believe that since most people in Latin America are of mixed race, there cannot be racism. While the amount of anti-black racism in Latin America may vary from country to country, they all have a common theme. Anti-black racism permeates society in Latin American countries, and it affects everyday life for Afro-Latinos, politically, socially, and economically.

We will examine the struggles Afro-Latinos face due to this racism and what is being done to combat systemic inequalities. In this book, we will look at the struggles faced by Afro-Latinos and their history in each Latin country.

Mexico

Afro-Mexicans have made contributions to Mexico that have been overlooked and ignored. Many people have yet to learn of the existence of Afro-Mexicans. According to Ismail Akwei (2019), Afro-Mexicans were first counted in Mexico's national survey in 2015 , where approximately 1.38 million people of African descent were counted, making up about 1.2% of Mexico's population. This is despite the fact that Spanish conquistadores sent approxitmately 200,000 enslaved Africans to Mexico in the 16th century (Kiko Martinez 2021). The fact it took this long for Afro-Mexicans to be recognized in their country shows how deeply embedded anti-black racism is in Mexico.

A lack of acknowledgment of people of African descent in Mexico is an attempt to erase their history and contributions. Of course, it is also a way to further marginalize them. This would inevitably make it more difficult for them to be represented in the media and politics.

Not being recognized as Mexican can lead to other more serious issues and bad experiences. They may be deported to other Latin American countries due to the fact that the police may not believe they are Mexican (Waweru 2018). Or as was in the case of Roshida Dowe (2022), she was the only person asked by Mexican immigration authorities for identification in a bus.

There are cases where, at military checkpoints, Afro-Mexicans may be asked to sing the National Anthem to prove they are Mexican (David Agren 2020). This is a terrible injustice and a gross form of racism Mexicans of African descent face. This form of racial profiling is deeply embedded in Mexican society. It is a way to make Afro-Mexicans invisible and not have recognition in their country. This lack of recognition is not helped by the fact many people may be inclined to believe their population has declined over the years. However, statistics indicate that the Afro-Mexican population is between two and eight percent of

Mexico's total population (Waweru 2018).

Mexicans need to become informed about AfroMexicans and the contributions of people of African descent in Mexico. People need to know that AfroMexicans exist and should not be treated as outsiders. With the help of activists, Afro-Mexicans will continue to receive more recognition and will likely receive more representation in politics, thus helping them to move up the economic and social ladder. They are a part of Mexico's contributions and helped build the nation.

They deserve more political and social representation. One of the biggest ironies about Mexican politics is that that country's second president, Vicente Guerrero, was a black man. He abolished slavery in Mexico in 1829 (Akwei 2019). The first free autonomous African community in the Americas was called San Lorenzo de los Negros, in what is today Yanga, named after Gaspar Yanga, who founded the municipality (Lara Villanueva 2022). The fact that you had a black man as Mexico's second president in their history and AfroMexicans not be recognized until just a few years ago shows how far the erasure of their history has gone.

Afro-Mexicans also helped establish Los Angeles in 1781 (Akwei 2019). Mexicans of African descent have made major contributions but are still fighting to be visible in their country. True "Mexican*ness*" has been associated with being "mestizaje," which is a racial and cultural mixture of Indigenous and Spaniard (Marycarmen Lara Villanueva 2022).

The "mestizaje" is the face of who Mexicans are to people in Mexico and the rest of the world. This may be why many of those who identify as Afro-Mexican also identify as Indigenous. According to Marycarmen Lara Villanueva (2022), two-thirds of those identifying as Afro-Mexican also identify as Indigenous. That may be due to the need to feel a sense of inclusion in Mexican society after remaining invisible for so long.

As Roshida Dowe (2022) said, race and socioeconomic status go hand in hand in Mexico. This racial hierarchy goes back to the times when Mexico was a Spanish colony, which had a colonial class system based on race (Lara Villanueva 2022). This encouraged race mixing in order for darker-skinned people to move up the economic and social ladder. It has kept Mexicans of African descent at the bottom of the social hierarchy in Mexico.

Afro-Mexicans were first counted in the census in 2020, which advocates note this inclusion in the census can help lead to advances (Lara Villanueva 2022). Increasing their visibility is important in addressing issues involving systemic discrimination and more inclusion in politics and economic gains. It can lead Mexicans who are of mixed race to acknowledge AfroMexicans and be open to giving them opportunities to be represented for them to achieve more social mobility.

The challenges Afro-Mexicans have to achieve social mobility are rather challenging. A survey performed by the National Council to Prevent Discrimination (CONAPRED) shows that a little more than 30% of Mexican men and women have little to no interest in seeing an Afro-Mexican president, while less than 25% of Mexican men and women would rent out a room to someone of African descent (Jasmin Aguilar Rangel 2022).

There is a widespread feeling in Mexican society that people of African descent do not belong or should not represent the country. They are not accepted in many realms of society, which is why they lag behind in political representation and being seen in Mexican media. The people of Mexico need to understand and be accepting of Afro-Mexicans as being part of Mexican society and culture. They are a part of the country's history. It is wrong for them to be excluded from many parts of Mexican society.

Many Afro-Mexicans are also denied access to basic rights or must do jobs that are considered to be theirs exclusively, such as agricultural work (Aguilar Rangel 2022). Afro-Mexicans are also less likely to have access to tap water and more likely to be illiterate (Aguilar Ranger 2022). They should be given the opportunities to receive rights and access to education and employment like other Mexicans. Not having access to opportunities will lead to them having a shorter life span and having a lower standard of living. There is a need to do away with racism in Mexico to achieve a more equal and fair society. Mexican society would rather keep them hidden and invisible so as to not deal with their racism. Identifying as black has been seen as being bad, though many young people are identifying as black, thus creating a glimmer of hope (Marina E. Franco 2022).

Perhaps the fact more people are embracing their blackness will lead to Afro-Mexicans having more visibility and representation. It will become normalized when people do not see blackness as a bad thing. Activists have called for affirming a black identity in the country as well as advocating for anti-racist school curricula (Lara Villanueva 2022). Doing this will definitely give Afro-Mexicans a voice and also will allow people to learn about Afro-Mexicans' contributions to the country and thus lead people to not look down on Afro-Mexicans. It will lead people to see blackness as being part of Mexican society.

There is a need to teach people about the role people of African descent have played in the history of Mexico. It will create black pride amongst AfroMexicans and eliminate a lot of the negativity associated with blackness. The Migration Policy Institute also recommends that immigration officials and public service agencies be provided with anti-discriminatory training in order to combat anti-black racism against black migrants (Lara Villanueva 2022).

Black migrants need to be treated fairly as well. Considering that Afro-Mexicans are often not believed by Mexican police to be of Mexican origin, it is very important for those who deal with the public and deal with immigration to be trained to treat black people fairly. Being that there has been an increase in black migrants in the country in recent years makes it all the more important in how Mexican authorities treat these migrants.

In recent years, African migrants have been detained in Tapachula, which is near the border with

Guatemala (S. Priya Morley 2021). They have suffered human rights abuses at the immigration center in Tapahula, which has led to the creation of the Assembly of African Migrants (Morley 2021).

It is important to address these types of abuses committed by Mexican authorities. There is a need to abolish racial profiling in cases involving African migrants and Afro-Mexicans. The country has to stop being in denial about its anti-black racism.

Part of the reason for the denial is the myth of "mestizaje," the idea that the people in the country all share the same mixed racial heritage, and therefore it is impossible or unlikely that it would motivate racial discrimination (Benjamin Russell 2020). Talking about racism in Mexico is taboo and creates resistance in public debate (Russell 2020). But the only way to dismantle racism is to confront it and not hide from it. Afro-Mexicans, as previously mentioned, lag behind in the social, economic, and political ladder. This has to change if Mexico is to see itself as a country with no racism. Increasing awareness of what is taking place in the country when it comes to racial injustices will go a long way to providing a platform for activists looking to bring changes. Giving activists a platform can also create a different portrayal of Afro-Mexicans and blackness as a whole. It can eliminate stereotypes and make people see a black identity in a positive manner.

Honduras

Honduras has a history of anti-black racism. Though Afro-Hondurans have been in Honduras for centuries, the country has tried to minimize or not acknowledge their existence. In the 1916 census, there were only two racial categories, indigenous and ladino (which was used for people of mixed race), and by 1920, racial categories had ceased to exist (Joshua Nadel 2014). It was not until 2001 that racial categories for people of African descent would be added to the census in Honduras (Nadel 2014). The fact that this was done in the census was to erase their presence and achievements in the development and culture of Honduras.

The idea of Mestizaje, a mix of European and Indigenous cultures, was used in the early 20th century to inspire national pride (Nadel 2014). This has left people of African descent at the bottom of the racial hierarchy. Black people in Honduras were seen as an impediment to Honduran society. This way of thinking in Honduran society has led to the marginalization of Afro-Hondurans and systemic discrimination. AfroHondurans are seen as less than those who are Mestizo and have more European features.

One group of Afro-Honduras is the Garifuna community. The Garifunas are a mixture of African slaves and the Carib Indigenous people on the island of what is today St. Vincent (John Dupuis 2016). The Garifunas experience serious human rights violations today in Honduras.

Massay Crisanto, a human rights activist in Honduras, says that the Garifuna community in Honduras is subject to violence (Human Rights Champions 2021). The Garifuna community is subject to land grabbing as well as attacks on their culture and people, and the government fails to protect them (Human Rights Champions 2021). This is a gross violation of their human rights and shows how far they are subjected to systemic racism. There is a need for activism to protect them from such human rights violations.

In Honduras, Afro hair is seen as negative, and Crisanto is looking to change that (Human Rights Champions 2021). European features in modeling are seen as more appealing. It is this deeply ingrained form of racism that allows for the government and society to not respect the rights of Afro-Hondurans. This creates the idea that it is okay to overlook the contributions made by the Garifuna community and other Afro Hondurans. Having an activist such as Crisanto will hopefully improve the situation for Afro-Hondurans. It is important to change the perception of Afro Hondurans.

There is a need to call attention as to what is happening to the Garifuna community, which is why Crisanto recently partnered with UN Human Rights (Human Rights Champions 2021). There have been calls for the disappearance of Garifuna leaders to be seriously investigated and for the leaders to be returned to their community (Brigida 2022). Those leaders should be allowed to return as they have done nothing wrong. If they are no longer alive, their families deserve closure, and so does their community.

The government of Honduras needs to heed the calls of the Garifuna community and human rights activists to seek justice for the attacks the community has endured. One such attack is by dispossession of land. Land ownership by the Garifunas became jeopardized during the 1990s when activities such as coastal tourism, housing, and palm oil production started taking place (Yanis Iqbal 2020).

The tourism industry has had an impact on the Garifuna community, where they are losing their livelihood. This is a terrible economic injustice. It is also a way of erasing the identity of the Garifunas. They use nature as part of their culture. Losing their ancestral territories will result in the Garifunas losing their identity, and they will cease to be a people (Iqbal 2020). Garifunas have a right to maintain their culture, land, and identity. They are in danger of losing who they are and what they have due to the development of their land by domestic and foreign investors.

Tragically, the laws implemented since the 1990s have allowed for them to be dispossessed. The government passed the 1992 Law for Modernization and Development of the Agricultural Sector, which promoted foreign and domestic investment in agriculture, and the Congressional Decree 90-90 supplemented this law by making foreigners eligible to purchase coastal lands (Iqbal 2020). The Honduran Constitution had previously restricted such a freeflowing movement of foreign capital, explicitly stating that only those who are Honduran-born may acquire or possess land or property along the coast (Iqbal 2020).

Activists have tried to make this injustice known across the country. Disenfranchising a group of people is a form of repression, being that Honduras clearly does not want people of African descent to thrive or be the face of their society. That is why anyone with African features is seen as being less than someone who is of mixed European and Indigenous culture. As the activist Missay Crisanto has stated, afro hair and dark skin are viewed in a negative light (Human Rights Champions 2021). The fact Afro-Hondurans are viewed this way means the government and society as a whole are not willing to fight for their rights, and many may advocate for their erasure as a people and culture.

The nation does not want them associated with Honduran society. It is an attempt to make them invisible. The idea that their skin color and hair are looked down upon is racist and will limit opportunities for them to participate in events such as a beauty pageant or perhaps even appear on Honduran TV.

The nation sees them as an obstacle to what it wants to do when it comes to agriculture and other economic developments. The government is willing to let foreigners develop the land at the expense of the Garifunas. They will allow any means necessary to terrorize the community. The fact that Honduras receives security assistance from Washington makes it even more challenging to mount a resistance (Miriam Miranda 2021).

The Garifunas will continue to face a struggle to maintain their communities due to the policies enacted. Those in power are doing everything for the Garifunas to lose this battle. The community lives in fear with all the backlash those in the community receive. There is a purge taking place there. Young people are leaving the community in droves due to the persecution and poor living conditions (Miranda 2021). This will inevitably lead to older people having to lead the struggle, but then the issue would be who would then live in the community?

The younger people who leave would not be there anymore to start families and pass down their land and culture to their descendants. This is an attempted genocide imposed by the Honduran government and investors. The youth need to be active in maintaining the land and culture their families and ancestors have lived on.

OFRANEH, the Black Fraternal Organization of Honduras, has been active in fighting for the Garifunas (Miranda 2021). They continue to make demands from the government to stop the dispossession. Even with all the threats of violence and persecution, OFRANEH does not back down. That organization, along with the

Garifunas have been resilient in fighting for their land and culture and will continue to do so.

Afro-Hondurans should not show any weakness against their government in seeking what rightfully belongs to them. They need to continue fighting against the exploitation of their land. Honduran society should also seek to integrate Afro-Hondurans without them having to give up their identity. They deserve to live safely without fear of persecution. It is also important for nature to be preserved, not just for the Garifunas living in those lands but also to preserve the ecosystem.

Laws should be passed for the Garifunas to receive protection for themselves and their land. It is important that activists make the situation of the Garifunas known to the rest of the country. Hopefully, creating awareness can help them bring change to the situation facing the Garifunas.

It is important also that Afro-Hondurans are not portrayed in a stereotypical manner through the media. Portraying Afro-Hondurans in a positive manner through the media can help in having their issues addressed more efficiently, as well as making it easier to integrate into Honduran society.

Promoting black pride will help in various ways as well. Not only will it perhaps encourage support in addressing their issues, but it will also allow for AfroHonduran models to be more easily accepted. It will open the door for Afro-Honduran models and may give them a major platform in beauty pageants in Honduras. Giving Afro-Hondurans a platform and creating representation can inspire change. The injustices against the Garifunas in Honduras need to stop and their rights should be respected.

Guatemala

Guatemala also has a Garifuna community along its coast. Livingston is where the Garifuna community in Guatemala exists (Amara Amaryah 2022). In the late 1970s, the Garifuna population in Livingston was around 10,000, and today, it is only around 4,000 (Amaryah 2022). They do face discrimination, and only a few port jobs exist in the town, as the town is controlled by Latin-owned businesses (Sarah Grainger 2009). This community is endangered of losing its identity because of these reasons.

Many Garifunas from Guatemala have moved to the United States, mostly to New York City (Grainger 2009). A lack of jobs has resulted in migration, and this migration means their culture and identity are at risk of being lost due to the fact it is not being maintained. Another reason for the previously mentioned migration was due to military recruitment during the civil war that took place from 1960 to 1996 (Scherly Virgill Artiaga

2020).

The experience of Garifunas has been omitted from the narrative of the country (Virgill Artiaga 2020). There needs to be recognition of the presence and experience the Garifunas have gone through in Guatemala. The Garifuna experience during the civil war in Guatemala has been erased. They have been made to be invisible in Guatemala.

According to a report by the Council on Hemispheric Affairs (2010), during the civil war, the Garifunas started to experience serious economic hardships. Those working in the docks of the coastal town of Puerto Barrios were laid off with the excuse that their company went bankrupt, but it was likely due to racism (COHA 2010). The fact they make up such a small percentage of Guatemala makes it easy to ignore the issues facing the Garifunas and not let the rest of the country know about their issues. Some may even not be aware of their existence.

Garifunas still struggle to attain their own institutions, and many Garifunas are politically apathetic (COHA 2010). This will inevitably make it more difficult for the Garifunas to make strides in Guatemala. There is this feeling that elected officials will do nothing for them. There are questions as to whether or not the Garifunas are overlooked compared to the Maya population (COHA 2010).

There have been efforts made for the progress of Garifunas. An organization called ASO-Garifuna was created to address issues facing the Garifunas and give Garifuna youth a voice (COHA 2010). There has been some notable progress made for Garifunas to be recognized in the country. The visibility of the Garifunas has increased through the government's Commission against Discrimination and Racism, which was led by a Garifuna who also held the post of Vice Minister of Culture, as well as the country celebrating *el dia del Garifuna* (Day of the Garifuna), which takes place on November 26th (COHA 2010).

This recognition may also lead to an increase in people self-identifying as Afro-Guatemalan. There is the belief that Afro-Guatemalans are undercounted due to biases inherent in self-reported identification (Ayah A. 2021). It is important for Afro-Guatemalans, and the Garifunas, to recognize their African ancestry and heritage in order to maintain their identity and culture. This will increase their visibility and allow for their stories to be told.

Many Guatemalans are unaware of their African ancestry due to the race-mixing and gradual assimilation into the Mestizo population (Ayah A. 2021). This is obviously more concerning for the Garifunas. As already mentioned, their culture and identity are in danger. Guatemalan society has already shown to not want to recognize people's African ancestry and not want to acknowledge the contributions and accomplishments of Afro-Guatemalans.

Despite attempts to have Garifunas assimilate, they have maintained their culture, including their dialect, music, cuisine, and spiritual beliefs (COHA 2010). Garifunas also value education, as their education level is higher than that of any indigenous group (COHA 2010). All of this shows resilience on the part of the Garifunas. They make the most of their situation to thrive and pass down their traditions to future generations despite the hardships and repression they face. It is important for them to maintain their culture and identity in order to prevent an erasure of the Garifunas in Guatemala.

The strides made by the Garifunas and Afro Guatemalans as a whole will hopefully create a better future for people of African descent in Guatemala. There needs to be more representation of Afro-Guatemalans in media, politics, education, and more in order to make their presence in the country known and to eliminate any stereotypes Guatemalan society has about Afro-Guatemalans.

There have been accomplishments made over the past two decades amongst Garifunas in Guatemala. Marva Weatherborn became Guatemala's first beauty queen of African descent in 2004, while Patricio Lorenzo became mayor of Livingston in 2008 (COHA 2010). Having an Afro-Guatemalan beauty queen is definitely of significance being that Guatemala, like other Latin American nations, values fair skin over dark skin. The accomplishment of Marva Weatherborn is a major milestone for Guatemala. Also, the fact that a Garifuna mayor was elected in a town with a large Garifuna population is important in order for the community to have someone who looks like them and can relate to them be in a position of power. The Afro Guatemalan population in the country may have a long struggle ahead, but they are making strides. They hope to create a better environment for future generations in the country.

Nicaragua

Nicaragua has long had an issue with anti-black racism in its country. This has led to some people not identifying as black, depending on what region of Nicaragua they are from. On the Caribbean coast, there is more of an acceptance of Afro identity due to the role of colonization and the proximity to Caribbean nations (Parker Diakite 2021). The two main groups of Afro-Nicaraguans along the Caribbean coast are the Creoles and the Garifunas (Diakite 2021).

There is a lack of acknowledgment of the contributions of Afro-Nicaraguans, especially in the Pacific and Central regions of the country (Diakite 2021).

This leads to the marginalization of Afro-Nicaraguans. They are treated as if they are not part of the country. Afro-Nicaraguans get asked for ID if they are traveling around the country, especially away from the Caribbean coast, due to an association between blackness and criminality (Diakite 2021).

These stereotypes create an environment of hostility towards Afro-Nicaraguans. This has led to a denial of blackness among some Afro-Nicaraguans. In the Pacific and Central regions, Afro-Nicaraguans are more likely to not identify as black due to the negative association of blackness (Diakite 2021). This negativity around blackness prevents Afro-Nicaraguans from fully engaging in Nicaraguan society.

People of African descent are barred from entry to certain spaces and schools (Nadra Nittle 2017). It does not help that people are in denial about the existence of racism. This prevents an honest dialogue on racism. There is an attempt to basically erase the culture of Afro-Nicaraguans. Creoles are not allowed to use their language in the workplace or at school, which leads to the danger of the language being lost (Nittle 2017).

Not many Nicaraguans know about the Caribbean coast, which leads many of them to assume that Afro-Nicaraguans are foreigners (Nittle 2017). There is the idea that everyone is a Mestizo, which is of mixed European and indigenous heritage (Nittle 2017). This creates an image that only a certain segment of society should be representative of the country. This is why when an Afro-Nicaraguan woman won Miss

Nicaragua in 2010, it was seen as a scandal due to the fact that she did not meet the European standard of beauty (Diakite 2021).

The country does not want people of African descent to take part in mainstream society or be the face of the country and its standard of beauty. There are many stereotypes that the country's black population has to overcome. It is terrible how they have to deal with outright discrimination and racism. There are reports of discrimination against black people at a hotel where a black family is bypassed by the hotel restaurant's owner and serves whites, and the black family leaves without being served (Nittle 2017).

There is a need for crackdowns and open dialogue on this type of racism in Nicaragua. There are too many instances of denial of acts of racism in the country. It appears that only when a major incident, such as the crowning of an Afro-Nicaraguan model as Miss Nicaragua or having the child of a politician denied entry to an establishment, is the issue of racism brought.

In 2009, the daughter of politician Bridgete Ivonne Budier Bryan was denied entry into a nightclub in the capital city of Managua, which prompted Bryan to call for the closure of the nightclub (Nittle 2017). The owners of the nightclub did eventually apologize but denied racism was the issue (Nittle 2017). This is indicative of how people are in denial of racism in Nicaraguan society.

The issue of denial of racism may have begun when Nicaragua gained its independence in 1821. That is when racial labels stopped being used for legal purposes in Western Nicaragua (Victoria GonzalezRivera 2020). The idea of not identifying Nicaraguans by race has benefited those of Spanish ancestry, whereas the idea of Nicaragua being a Mestizo nation has been a powerful and seductive one (GonzalezRivera 2020). It has allowed the majority of

Nicaraguans to deny racism being an issue in the country. They may also engage in acts of anti-black racism and treat it as the norm.

In Nicaragua, it has become the norm to use racialized nicknames such as "chele" or "chela" (Gonzalez-Rivera 2020). This leads to the issue of lacking self-love when you are Afro-Nicaraguan. There has been some progress for recognition made over the years.

The Sandinistas passed the autonomy law in 1987, which officially recognized the black populations in the North and South Caribbean Coast Autonomous Regions (Wawen Ewimbi 2022). The Autonomous Regions were created after the British vacated Nicaragua in the 1850s, and the emancipated Africans then formed their own multi-lingual, multi-cultural, and communally economic society (Nefta Freeman 2021). The fact that the Sandinistas support recognition of the African populations in the Autonomous Regions inevitably leads to strong support from the African populations.

There is a saying that "Autonomy is the revolution (Freeman 2021). It is important that AfroNicaraguans continue to fight for recognition and equality. The racism in Nicaragua will have their identity and culture erased if there is no resistance.

As activist William Mina has said, "AfroNicaraguans are motivated to fight by their culture and tradition so that the children of Afro-Nicaraguans can live in tranquility (Nittle 2017)."

Afro-Nicaraguans have been shown to be resilient in fighting for justice. They have been met with challenges even from abroad. The U.S. government has sought to undermine what the Sandinistas have done to help Afro-Nicaraguans by funding the Contras in the 1980s and even in more recent years of stirring up a violent campaign of terror (Freeman 2021).

It is tragic that the black population in Nicaragua has to deal with issues that hinder their progress both inside Nicaragua and from an outside influence. Fortunately, the Sandinistas remain very popular in Nicaragua, with a 72% approval rating as recently as

2016 (Freeman 2021). Hopefully, this will allow Afro-Nicaraguans to continue making strides in the country.

Afro-Nicaraguans should be allowed to express black pride and be allowed to assimilate into Nicaraguan society without losing their culture and identity. The authorities should not be profiling AfroNicaraguans to where they are assumed to be criminals.

There needs to be awareness and training for AfroNicaraguans not to be unfairly targeted by the authorities. The country should teach about the history and contributions that people of African ancestry have made to Nicaragua.

The United States government needs to stay out of the affairs of Nicaragua. Any interference or overthrow of the Nicaraguan government led by the Sandinistas will probably set back any gains made by Afro-Nicaraguans. Normalizing black beauty in Nicaragua will lead to more of an acceptance of AfroNicaraguans winning beauty pageants without the country having a negative reaction.

The government should protect the rights of Afro-Nicaraguans as well as their culture and language. The country should be open to having dialogues on racism. The only way to eliminate the problem of racism is to talk about it and seek solutions to abolish it. AfroNicaraguans are seeking to secure a better future for their children and grandchildren.

The government should set up quotas in order to increase the representation of Afro-Nicaraguans in different job sectors. A quota system could lead to an increase in the acceptance and embrace of their African heritage and roots. It will lead many to identify as black. Nicaragua needs to have a positive portrayal of blackness in the media, which also will help in increasing black pride and acceptance as part of Nicaraguan society.

El Salvador

El Salvador is a nation that has African influence and mixture in its culture and population, but most people in the country are unaware of this. El Salvador is the only Central American nation that does not have a Garifuna, Miskito, or Afro-Antillean population (Kent C. Williams 2018). This may be the reason why the African influence in this country may be overlooked or ignored.

Most people in El Salvador will claim their country is the only Central American country without a black population (Williams 2018). The reason why there are no African people in El Salvador is due to the fact that there was inter-racial mixing going back over 400 years where the African origins are unknown, even to those who have such a background (Williams 2018). This race mixing has led to a country without a black identity in its population.

The country also, at one time, banned black people from immigrating to El Salvador (Williams 2018).

This would obviously prevent a black presence from existing in the country, being that the African origins of its population were diluted. People of African descent have been erased from El Salvadorian society. Less than .1% of El Salvador's total population is black, which is why questions about the black population were no longer included in the country's census (OHCHR 2006).

Though there is no recognized black identity in the country, there is African influence. There is an African influence in the national folk instrument, the marimba (Williams 2018). Salvadorian popular music and Afro-Caribbean rhythms and dances have African influences (Williams 2018). El Salvador is one country without a very significant black population, so there is no true defined black experience in the country.

As Williams (2018) reports, the El Salvadorian's identity is not based on race or ethnicity but rather on just being El Salvadorian. Being that there is no black presence in El Salvador, there is nothing to show how people of African descent would be treated in the country. But being that black immigration was banned at one time , it is obvious that black people would probably be marginalized if they did exist in the country.

What there needs to be is training and education about the contributions of people of African descent to the culture. Even though a black identity has been erased in the country, the people of El Salvador should be aware of the influence people of African descent have had in their society.

Costa Rica

IN Costa Rica today, Afro-Costa Ricans make up about 8% of the country's population (Bruno Bragga 2021). The first black population arrived in Costa Rica in the 16 century as slaves (Bragga 2021). Most black people who later arrived in Costa Rica migrated there to seek a better life and employment (Carter Maddox 2021). They would eventually be left without access to employment or prohibited from traveling to the highlands due to laws being passed (Maddox 2021). They were not recognized as citizens until 1949, when a new Constitution was written following a civil war where black people fought to enjoy rights as citizens (Nduta Waweru 2018). This still did not prevent them from experiencing discrimination in the country.

In the 1950s, some Afro-Costa Ricans were allowed to obtain ID and seek employment though they were confined to one region (Maddox 2021). Racism has made Afro-Costa Ricans do certain things to deny or erase their blackness. By the late 1970s, about 6% of Afro-Costa Ricans had married white Costa Ricans in an effort to have better access to social or economic mobility (Maddox 2021). The need for AfroCosta Ricans to do this is a way to erase their identity from Costa Rican society. It has caused them to feel invisible in the country. More needs to be done for their existence, history, and culture to be recognized. The struggle they face has inevitably led to tension in the country. Today there is conflict between blacks and whites in Costa Rica (Maddox 2021).

There needs to be a constructive and serious discussion about systemic racism in Costa Rica. AfroCosta Ricans tend to work the lowest-paying jobs and in the poorest conditions (Maddox 2021). There is a lack of opportunity for Afro-Costa Ricans, which has created economic inequality in the country. Because of this, many have migrated to the United States (Maddox 2021).

There is also the issue of a disparity in the health care system. There are health issues that mainly affect

Afro-Costa Ricans, but health professionals are often reluctant to discuss prevention treatments (Maripaz Soto Villalobos 2022). Having a population that is emigrating will make it harder for them to gain visibility in Costa Rica, as they will have fewer people who can fight their struggle. It may also make it more difficult for them to maintain their customs and traditions.

Costa Rica has erased most of the ancestral black knowledge, and there are no written records due to the fact their legacy was collected orally, being that Afro-Costa Ricans were not provided with proper written education (Soto Villalobos 2022). It is a tragedy that the country's blackness is not recognized as it should be. The country has to confront its history of racism in order to resolve racial tensions in the country.

One way that Afro-Costa Ricans look to fight for equality is by expressing themselves in the parade for "Day of Black People and Afro-Costa Rican Culture." This parade in the city of Limon is a way to commemorate the struggles of Afro-Costa Ricans as well as the identities that have been formed and the contributions the city has made to the country and the Caribbean region (Soto Villalobos (2022). This is an opportunity for them to make demands and seek improvements in the lives of Afro-Costa Ricans. The country has emphasized whiteness in the country, which is one reason the Afro-Costa Rican community is neglected.

The country has never considered itself a Caribbean country because it would rather see itself as the "Central American Switzerland" (Soto Villalobos 2022). Costa Rica has embraced the myth of being a white nation, a white middle-class nation with closer links to Europe than Central America (Silvia Alonso 2021). This fact has made it obvious as to why AfroCosta Ricans have been historically marginalized. The country does not want them to give them a voice or representation. They would rather ignore the fact that there is a black population in the country.

The main problem facing Costa Rica in regard to anti-black racism is the fact that there is a denial of racism in the country (Alonso 2021). A country denying its racism problems will never resolve them. Costa Rican society needs to have a dialogue on what it needs to do to end racism. Continuously silencing the voice of Afro-Costa Ricans will only maintain the status quo and thus continue the problem.

Through all of this, progress is being made. In 2018, Costa Rica elected a black woman vice president for the first time in the country's history (Damola Durosomo 2018). It is a first not only for Costa Rica but for all of Latin America (Durosomo 2018). Hopefully, this will increase the visibility of the country's black population. The first black woman vice president, Epsy Campbell Barr, mentioned building a more inclusive society for everyone to benefit (Durosomo 2018). Hopefully, this will inspire others to do more to help in the struggle for Afro-Costa Ricans.

What can also help Afro-Costa Ricans is the fact that there are black Americans moving to the Caribbean coast of Costa Rica. Many black Americans have moved to Costa Rica to escape the racism they face in America (Alaysia Lane 2022). Black Americans will experience a level of privilege in Costa Rica, being that they speak English and have US currency, allowing them to live in the nicer areas of the country, but they are still not exempt from experiencing racism (Lane 2022).

The fact there is a black American presence in Costa Rica may help Afro-Costa Ricans because black Americans have historically fought against anti-black racism the most. Learning about the history of black Americans can inspire and give hope to the fight against anti-black racism in Costa Rica.

The country should address the issues and inequalities it faces due to race. They should teach about the history of black slaves in Costa Rica. Most Costa Ricans did not know there was slavery in the country that lasted from 1502 to 1824 (Lane 2022). This level of ignorance makes it easier to dismiss the issues facing Afro-Costa Ricans. It means there will be less understanding as to how Afro-Costa Ricans are at the point they are currently at, and it will eliminate any sympathy from the rest of Costa Rican society.

It is important that Costa Ricans are made aware of the struggles that Afro-Costa Ricans have faced in order for dialogues to take place and policies put in place to help Afro-Costa Ricans. Having elected officials of African descent helps that others can look to them as symbols of hope and change in an unequal society.

Panama

anama is a country that may be located in Central America but, politically and historically, is not considered Central America. It is also a country that has issues with anti-black racism. There is a struggle to promote Afro pride. In a report where a young Afro-Panamanian lady was interviewed, she had struggled throughout her childhood and adolescence but has now finally managed to embrace her Afro heritage (Astrid Chang 2021).

In Panama, discrimination and segregation of Afro-Panamanians have created an environment where people of African descent and African features are looked down upon. There are movements to create awareness of anti-black racism and to promote pride in African heritage. An activist named Nina Ottey is helping lead that movement with her platform "Menina Congo," which empowers Afro-Panamanian women (Chang 2021).

In her platform, she will talk about different

topics, including rejection because of hair texture which sometimes leads to employment discrimination (Chang 2021). The fact that hair texture can lead to discrimination in the workplace means that Afro-Panamanians will further increase poverty rates in the Afro community. This obviously leads to Afro-Panamanians looking down on themselves and not wanting to be associated with blackness.

As Nina Ottey stated, many Panamanians are ashamed of their African ancestry (Chang 2021). That is why she also integrates an event called "Melanie Summer Fest," where Afro-Panamanian women come together in the summer to discuss culture, self-discovery, and Afro-hair, along with other topics (Chang 2021). It appears that despite Afro-Panamanians being visible in the country, they ar encouraged to restrict their visibility. There are other factors that can further hinder anti-black discrimination. In a study done in 2020, it was found that AfroPanamanians can suffer other forms of discrimination along with being black, such as discrimination due to age, sex, language, religion, political, social origin, property, disability, birth, or other condition (Chang 2021). These other forms of discrimination make it more difficult for many Afro-Panamanians to seek equality. It further disenfranchises them.

Afro-Panamanian women, in particular, suffer from double discrimination due to race and gender or triple discrimination when you add poverty (Chang 2021). Even when Afro-Panamanian women have higher levels of education, on average, they earn less and have higher unemployment rates (Chang 2021). Evidence of the inequality is present in the district of Curundu, which is the second largest district of Afro- Panamanians in Panama City (Javier Wallace 2020).

There is a lot of poverty in this section of Panama City. In this district, two men have co-founded an organization called Asosacion Deportiva Curundu (ADC), which seeks to address issues facing the community by using sports and workshops for the youth (Wallace 2020) . This organization is a much-needed entity in a country with so much racial inequality.

Afro-Panamanian men are often stereotyped as criminals and experience abuse from law enforcement (Wallace 2020). It is important that Afro-youth are taught what to do when dealing with law enforcement and also to guide them in order for them to avoid becoming a statistic. The co-founders of ADC, Cesar Santos, and Andres Madrid, created the organization to teach the youth about the rules of life (Wallace 2020). Being that the co-founders know what it is like to grow up black and impoverished in Panama, they can relate to the youth and help them improve their situation. They can teach them their rights when dealing with the police. This is imperative in a country where poor Afro-Panamanian males are murdered by police officials and in correctional facilities (Wallace 2020).

Panama needs institutional changes to address its anti-black discrimination. They should train their law enforcement officials how to better interact with

AfroPanamanians. The hair texture of Afro-Panamanians should be seen as normal, and thus, people of African descent experience discrimination over that. This is a way to attack their identity and culture. They should be allowed to integrate into Panamanian society without having to compromise their culture.

It is important that people also learn about the contributions black people made in Panama. Black people in Panama have inherited customs from West Africa, and it shows in their music, dances, customs, language, gastronomy, religion, outfits, and hairstyles, which they have brought to Panama (Brunno Braga 2022). They have enriched Panama with these cultural traits. They also made contributions during the Colonial Era as well as during the construction of the railway and Canal (Braga 2022).

Making Panamanian society aware of the contributions made by Afro-Panamanians can only help them in their struggle for equality. It will give them acknowledgment, thus preventing an erasure of their culture and identity. It can help bridge the wealth gap between Afro-Panamanians with the rest of the country. Teaching people about the contributions made by Afro-Panamanians can help eliminate stereotypes about them. It will make it easier for integration and also have others acknowledge their struggle and historical grievances.

Having Black American expats living in Panama can also help as black Americans' struggles against racism have influenced other people of African ancestry around the world. It can inspire AfroPanamanians to continue struggling for an end to racism and increase the feeling of black pride.

Colombia

Colombia is a country with a significant black population. It is a country wreaked by violence towards Afro-Colombians. In regions of Colombia that have predominantly black populations, such as Choco, you have high poverty rates (James Baldwin 2020). The problems facing these regions are exacerbated by left-wing guerrilla groups and right-wing paramilitary groups looking to control the drug trade and arms trafficking in the region (Baldwin 2020). There is also large-scale corporate mining by foreign companies as well as illegal mining by armed groups (Baldwin 2020).

A situation like this makes it impossible for the local Afro-Colombian community to make gains. The Colombian state does not make it a priority to protect the local black population and to help them when they have issues such as disastrous floods due to heavy rain (Baldwin 2020). They are a neglected community. They need help from the government but do not receive it.

Their land is being used for purposes other than helping the local economy of these communities. This is despite the fact that the 1991 Constitution, along with declaring Colombia a multi-cultural and multiethnic society, also recognized territorial autonomies and designated political representation for Afro-Colombians (Steven Cohen 2014).

On paper, Afro-Colombians may have legal protections, but in reality, not much is done to enforce these protections. The neglect of Afro-populated regions in Colombia has led to mass migration to major urban areas, where Afro-Colombians are subject to various forms of racism and discrimination (Cohen 2014). There is also the issue of institutionalized racism, which enables the Afro-Colombian population to be undercounted.

In a 2018 census, it stated that three million people in Colombia identified themselves as being of African descent though some activists put that number much higher so that it reflected that 15% to 20% of Colombia is of African descent (Manuel Rueda 2021). In that census, it was estimated that 30% of Afro-Colombians lack access to adequate housing, basic schooling, and formal employment (Rueda 2021). Race and socioeconomic status go hand in hand in Colombia. As mentioned about the regions such as Choco, the violence from militias has led to the displacement of black populations in those affected regions. Another problem that makes it harder to fix this issue is that the black identity in Colombia is not recognized. Despite having the second largest African population in South America after Brazil, this racial identity is not embraced, acknowledged, and celebrated as it is in Brazil (Shahida Muhammad 2015).

In a country where over 85% of the population identifies as being of "no ethnicity," it is hard to speak about race when race in Colombian society, for the most part, is not seen as a concept (Muhammad 2015). This denial of race and identity makes it easy to deny any racial divisions and the social and economic impact it has on society. The inequalities are present, but Colombian society pretends race is not a factor.

Colombia needs to give a voice to the Afro population in the country. The election of Colombia's first black vice president can perhaps bring some progress. Francia Marquez became the first black vice president in Colombian history when her running mate, Gustavo Petro, took office as the president in August 2022 (Associated Press 2022).

Marquez was an environmental activist who, due to her work, faced death threats and is also seen as different than any vice president in the country's history due to the way she was raised (Associated Press 2022). This may be what Colombia needs to make progress when it comes to racism (and other inequalities) facing the country.

People living in rural areas and those of African ancestry identify with her, which is why her running mate won big among the Afro-Colombian population living on the Pacific coast (Associated Press 2022). Hopefully, Afro-Colombians will achieve substantial gains and not just a symbolic gesture by having a black vice president in office.

Afro-Colombians should receive protection from the government in regard to facing violence from militias. The legal protections offered to them need to be enforced. It only makes it more difficult for Afro-Colombians to overcome racism if the legal protections offered to them are not enforced.

The 1991 Constitution brought a change in how Colombia saw itself; it had previously seen itself as a homogenous culture and society (Ana Margarita Gonzales 2012). Being recognized as an ethnic minority allows Afro-Colombians to address their issues. However, not enforcing any policies or laws prevents any true substantive changes from taking place. Global networks, multilateral organizations, international conventions and norms, and foundations have all been proven to be essential in the attempt to make the country more inclusive and humane (Gonzalez 2012). There are obviously still many obstacles that Colombia has to overcome to abolish systemic racism. They need to make the country aware of the contributions of Afro-Colombians. They need to have their land protected because if not, it can lead to the erasure of their culture and history. The only way Colombia can be truly inclusive towards Afro-Colombians is by maintaining the identity of Afro-Colombians.

The dangers faced by Afro-Colombians mean they face the strong possibility of not having the resources needed to rise above poverty. They will be left with nothing and thus not be able to achieve the goals of seeking equality in a country with anti-black racism. They also need to be accepting of people who are of a darker complexion.

In Colombian culture, it is more common for women to have straight, long, and light-colored hair (Rachel George 2019). An Afro-Colombian journalist once received backlash for wearing her hair in its natural curly state (George 2019). The fact that anything associated with blackness is seen as a negative needs to change.

Gaining acceptance and recognition is important for Afro-Colombians to achieve equality. Afro-Colombian culture is seen in the music and dances of Colombia, such as reggaeton, cumbia, champeta, jazz, and other genres (George 2019). The fact that their culture is ingrained in Colombian society will help enable them to preserve their identity. It can be a way to express their goals and needs. It can inspire hope and aspiration for future generations.

Colombia is still a long way from achieving racial harmony, but the resilience and creativity of Afro-Colombians to make gains and maintain their culture goes a long way, especially when faced with violence and other threats.

Ecuador

Ecuador is a country with systemic racism against people of African descent. According to a human rights group, the government of Ecuador needs to step up to end racial discrimination against Afro-Ecuadorians and protect them (OHCHR 2019). Afro-Ecuadorians have disproportionate rates of poverty and lack access to necessities to make a decent living, including the lack of clean water, land, security, justice, healthcare, and economic opportunity (OHCHR 2019). These problems create terrible suffering for Afro-Ecuadorians. These issues need to be addressed to create a fairer society in Ecuador.

It is inhumane for this population to face such human rights abuses and discrimination. In Esmeraldas, the province with the highest Afro population in Ecuador, Afro-Ecuadorians have a poverty rate of 85% along with a 15% illiteracy rate and only 23% having access to the most basic services (OHCHR 2019). These numbers are staggering. This is an indicator of the extreme suffering they experience.

There are activists fighting anti-black racism, including subtle forms of anti-black racism. Catherine Chala, founding member of the National Coordinator for Black Women in Ecuador, is fighting against racism and sexism towards Afro-Ecuadorian women (Valerie Carmel 2018). Afro-women who studied to become nurses or accountants could not work in those fields due to discrimination (Carmel 2018).

It is tragic that systemic and institutionalized racism prevents them from accessing those types of jobs. This will discourage Afro-women (and men) from seeking certain jobs, which will further hinder social mobility. In the province of Esmeraldas, Afro-Ecuadorians are affected by industries trying to take over their land, where the Afro population may have their families threatened if they refuse to sell to those in certain industries (Carmel 2018). This attempt to dispossess Afro-Ecuadorians of their land is another form of injustice and racial discrimination they face in their country. This is why Chala continues to organize in order to combat racism. And the racism can come in subtle forms.

Chala mentions there are Afro-Ecuadorian women who do not want to identify as black or Afro-Ecuadorian (Carmel 2018). This denial of black identity is an attempt to avoid being impacted by racial discrimination and systemic racism. It is an attempt to not confront the issue of racism, but it is obviously not a way to abolish systemic racism in Ecuador.

There have also been instances of people being upset at who represents the country on an international scale. Over the last two decades, the Ecuadorian soccer team has represented the country in the World Cup, where the majority of the players are Afro-Ecuadorians (O. Hugo Benavides 2017). There have been three Afro-Ecuadorian women to represent Ecuador in the Miss Universe pageant and other international events going back to the mid-90s (Benavides 2017). These achievements have not taken place without objections from many Ecuadorians.

One caller to a radio station stated that people

would believe Ecuador is a black country, whose tone of voice implied that it would not be a good thing (Benavides 2017). There is racial anxiety in regard to how Ecuador will be represented on the international level.

When it comes to the national soccer team, it is not a problem to have black players represent the country as long as the team is winning (Benavides 2017). There is the idea that blacks are naturally gifted athletically, so if the soccer team wins, they are hailed as being naturally superior athletically, and if they lose, they are seen as naturally inferior and stupid (Benavides 2017).

There is obviously a need to teach the people of Ecuador tolerance towards people of African descent. They need to do away with stereotypes about Afro-Ecuadorians and be willing to give them jobs they are qualified for. People need to be made aware of the contributions Afro-Ecuadorians have made to the culture of Ecuador. The government should step up to protect the rights of Afro-Ecuadorians and make sure they are given opportunities to help them overcome the disproportionate poverty they face.

Making people aware of Afro-Ecuadorian culture will help lead to black pride and thus make it more likely for people to identify as Afro-Ecuadorian. This can only reduce the chances that people will be concerned about how Ecuador is portrayed and seen on a global scale.

An increase in Afro-Ecuadorian representation on an international level will only normalize that and will influence Ecuadorian society to be more accepting and tolerant towards people of African descent. The country may perhaps look to set up quotas in universities and in the workplace to create more opportunities for Afro-Ecuadorians and give them more visibility.

Peru

Peru is a nation whose society deals with stereotypes about people of African descent. Newspaper tabloids and TV programs abound with stereotypes to the point where people do not question them due to becoming so familiar with them (Dan Collyns 2010). When people complain about these stereotypes being reinforced, they are often met with remarks such as asking where is people's sense of humor (Collyns 2010). The fact that something like this is seen as a joke makes it harder to get over these stereotypes and give Afro-Peruvians fair treatment.

If a TV show depicts Afro-Peruvians in an offensive manner, then they may be told to simply change the channel if they do not like what they see. These stereotypes ingrained in Peruvian society, of course, make it more difficult for Afro-Peruvians to move up the social ladder.

Most Afro-Peruvians are trapped in poverty and lack opportunities, as they earn, on average, 40% less than mixed-race people (Collyns 2010). Afro-Peruvians can also be seen as less intelligent academically. Carmen Luz Medrano, a school teacher in El Carmen, which is a historic population centre of Afro-Peruvians, said that when she was going to school, the teachers would say that black people could only think until midday (Collyns 2010). Any teacher who thinks this way is obviously not going to be fair to any Afro-Peruvian student and can damage an Afro-Peruvian's student confidence and self-esteem. It will also lead to some Afro-Peruvians denying their blackness.

As Cecilia Ramirez, director of the Peruvian Black Women's Development Centre, has stated being that black is associated with everything bad and negative, the children of Afro-Peruvian parents are negatively impacted psychologically by discrimination that they want to deny their black identity and heritage (Collyns 2010). The irony of the low self-esteem and denial of black identity is that Afro-Peruvians have contributed a lot to Peruvian society.

Peruvian culture has been influenced by the

music, dance, food, and religious festivals of Afro-Peruvians (Collyns 2010). Their influence is strong, considering they make up around just 3% of Peru's total population (Jimmy J. De La Cruz 2019). Being that Afro-Peruvians make up such a low percentage of the country's population means that the country's black population can stand out or be made to feel invisible. Their history is not taught in the schools in Peru (De La Cruz 2019). This will obviously lead to people in the country being unaware of the contributions Afro-Peruvians have made. It further creates low self-esteem for Afro-Peruvian school children. And when they are represented in the media, they are often portrayed in a negative light (De La Cruz 2019).

There is a need to give Afro-Peruvians a positive voice and image in the country. The media will portray Afro-Peruvian men as criminals or full of aggression, while minstrel shows will have actors dress up in blackface portraying Afro-Peruvians in a stereotypical manner (De La Cruz 2019). This has led to Afro-Peruvian advocacy groups calling for the removal of stereotypical characters from Peruvian TV shows though they are still being televised (De La Cruz 2019). It is obvious that the country needs to address its racist attitudes. Depicting Afro-Peruvians in a positive light in the media would be one way to start adjusting the attitudes against Afro-Peruvians.

In 2009, Peru became the first country in the region to apologize for the centuries of mistreatment of people of African descent (Collyns 2010). However, this is not enough. Many steps should be taken to address racism and change people's attitudes in Peru. It would be just as important to teach school-aged children the contributions and history of Afro-Peruvians. This will reduce the chances of a teacher seeing an Afro-Peruvian student as less academically gifted.

Afro-Peruvians need to be assimilated into Peruvian society. They need to be given access to wealth and better living conditions. Mainstream TV programs should not be allowed to depict Afro-Peruvians in an offensive and stereotypical manner. The government should look to establish quotas in order for Afro-Peruvians to be represented, especially in government and other positions of power. They should look to educate people to not see Afro-Peruvians in a stereotypical manner, especially with the men being portrayed as criminals.

The country needs to take issues of racism seriously and not simply dismiss them as a joke. Making a joke out of racism will only make it harder to address racism and will even lead to more people seeing Afro-Peruvians in a stereotypical and unfair manner. They should give people bias training in order to not be intolerant of Afro-Peruvians. Afro-Peruvians should be given access to healthcare without fear of being discriminated against. A lot of work needs to be done in order to eliminate racism and have Afro-Peruvians assimilated into Peruvian society.

Bolivia

Bolivia is a country where anti-black racism has led to the near complete erasure of the history of Afro-Bolivians in the country. Afro-Bolivians have been largely ignored in the country though strides have been made in recent years for Afro-Bolivians to obtain legal protection and acknowledgment. Most Afro-Bolivians are descendants of slaves brought to the country in the mid-16th century (Olivia Hylton-Pennant 2015).

After slavery was abolished in 1851, hacienda owners in the Yungas region, where most descendants of African slaves in Bolivia live today, would exploit Afro-Bolivians until the agrarian reform of 1953 (Hylton-Pennant 2015). Despite this, Afro-Bolivians would still experience discrimination in the country, and the government would ignore them (HyltonPennant 2015).

It is clear that Afro-Bolivians have faced a tough struggle throughout Bolivia's history. Activists have fought to bring reform to Bolivia in order to help the causes of Afro-Bolivians. Some strides made include the introduction of Law 200 in 2011, which included the requisite that Afro-Bolivians be recognized on the census after they had been omitted for over 100 years (Hylton-Pennant 2015).

Being included in the census will give AfroBolivians recognition and allow their voices to be heard. This can help them make progress in obtaining equality. Article 32 of the Bolivian Constitution in 2009 also states that Afro-Bolivians enjoy the economic, political, social, and cultural rights recognized in the Constitution for the nations and rural Native Indigenous people (Hylton-Pennant 2015). This is a major step for Afro-Bolivians in achieving equality and recognition.

In 2010, Afro-Bolivian leader Jorge Medina was elected to the Bolivian parliament, making him the country's first-ever Afro-Bolivian deputy to serve in the country's parliament (Hylton-Pennant 2015). Of course, it will take hard work in order to obtain equality and proper recognition of Afro-Bolivians. No other Afro-Bolivians have been elected to parliament since Medina in 2010 (Hylton-Pennant 2015).

Another leader who is fighting the struggle is King Julio Pinedo, who is the head of the Afro-Bolivian monarchy in the Yungas region (Aleksa Vuckovic 2021). He pushes ahead, creating hope for Afro-Bolivians. He has a huge responsibility made more difficult by the poverty in Bolivia. Afro-Bolivians get hit the hardest with issues dealing with education, employment, health care, and more, making it more of a challenge (Vuckovic 2021). King Pinedo understands his role where he knows he is not rich like kings in Europe but knows that representing the Afro-Bolivian community is a big responsibility, and his duties include resolving disputes between Afro- Bolivians (Vuckovic 2021).

Though Afro-Bolivians are seeing an increase in recognition, they are far from being properly represented in government and other sectors of Bolivian society. The government should establish quotas to increase Afro-Bolivian representation in government and other public sectors. The government should seek to enforce the policies in Article 32 of the Bolivian Constitution in order for Afro-Bolivians to obtain what is supposed to be guaranteed in the Constitution.

There needs to be an increase in visibility for Afro-Bolivians. The fact that King Pinedo and his wife were crowned in 2007 by the governor of La Paz is a milestone (Jordi Busque 2021). This would give them recognition throughout the country. Having King Pinedo travel to Uganda to become more aware of his roots is also important (Busque 2021). Something like that would help create black pride and also make other Afro-Bolivians trace back their African roots.

All of this will help preserve and recognize the identity of Afro-Bolivians. It is just as important to pass down the knowledge of their roots to future generations. Allowing Afro-Bolivians to have recognition in the country is important to have their issues addressed and for them to be assimilated into Bolivian society. They are a remarkable group of people who have maintained their culture and have knowledge of their history when the rest of the country made them invisible. They should be given access to better living conditions and employment. They should be assimilated into Bolivian society. The knowledge of their ancestors will help give them inspiration to keep up the struggle as they would like for their children to have a better future.

Chile

Chile is a country with a lot of anti-black racism. Chile is a nation with a whitewashed identity. The Afro-Chilean community has long been a scapegoat for various social problems in the country (Gabriela Mesones Rojo 2020). Migrants of African descent are also marginalized in the country. There are protections and benefits for migrants from Europe, while racialized migrants are seen as a threat to the supposed order and security of the country (Mesones Rojo 2020).

It is clear that Chile has an environment of xenophobia towards people of African descent. AfroChileans have also not been acknowledged on the national census (Maya Doig-Acuna 2020). Throughout its history, the country has tried to deny the existence of black people. The country has made it virtually impossible to be Chilean with a black identity. Erasure and dismissal are two challenges in dealing with the recognition of Afro-Chileans (Doig-Acuna 2020). Black immigrants also experience structural racism and are targets of anti-immigration sentiment (Doig-Acuna 2020). The country has to improve in how they treat people of African descent.

There is some hope for change. A new law granting legal recognition to Afro-Chileans was established in 2019 (Boris van der Spek 2019). This may lead Chilean society to acknowledge the culture and contributions of Afro-Chileans to the country. The fact they have been invisible is ironic based on the history of Chile.

When Chile was explored by Diego de Almagro, the Afro population was 13 % (Van der Spek 2019). Various infantries regiments of the Liberation Army of Bernardo O'Higgins that fought the Spanish Empire consisted entirely of black men (Van der Spek 2019). Slavery is also part of the history of Afro-Chileans and it was in part due to black people that slavery was made illegal in 1823 (Van der Spek 2019). One way that can make the Afro-Chilean community more visible is by educating people about them.

As Chilean lawmaker Luis Rocafull said, "In school, they were honoring their European-looking founding fathers while ignoring the roles and contributions of those of African descent (Parker Diakite, 2022)."

Making people aware of the existence and contributions of Afro-Chileans throughout Chilean history is a major step in Afro-Chileans gaining recognition in the country. They, of course, would also like to get respect. Even though there is no issue of Afro-Chileans being killed by law enforcement or other violent acts of racism, they are still fighting to be treated properly and fairly (Diakite 2022). There may be a child being picked on or bullied in school due to their skin color (Diakite 2022). This type of behavior should be called out since it is wrong and unfair to be treated like this due to one's skin color.

Chile has been transitioning into a democracy from a dictatorship going back 30 years; the Constitution has been changing (Diakite 2022). This is an opportunity for the issues affecting Afro-Chileans to be addressed. They can have rights embedded into the changing Constitution. They can have the census recognize them as an ethnic group in Chile. Their cause has also been helped by immigration from people of African descent.

There have been a lot of immigrants to Chile in the past 20 years who came from countries such as Brazil, Haiti, Colombia, Uruguay, Ecuador, and Venezuela, and that has created a necessity to know about the diaspora (Diakite 2022). This need to know about the diaspora can further help Afro-Chileans gain recognition, being that the country will have to acknowledge the existence of people of African descent in the country. It will create curiosity and may have people wanting to know more about Afro-Chileans.

The fact that there are black immigrants will make it necessary for the country to respect their rights. Those rights will benefit Afro-Chileans as well as black immigrants. It is important people acknowledge the contributions of Afro-Chileans. Historically, scholars have looked to erase the history and contributions of Afro-Chileans in the country (Mark Newman 2022). However, in the last decade, scholars have worked to retrieve Afro-Chilean history through archives and oral history as a way to counter the myth of erasure (Newman 2022).

The fact that there had been attempts to erase the history of Afro-Chileans shows how deeply embedded racism is in Chile. The history of AfroChileans should be taught in school. Not teaching the history of Afro-Chileans can only lead to the erasure of the culture and identity. It can also erase the existence of black immigrants in Chile (Newman, 2022). But activists are making sure that the identity of AfroChileans will gain more recognition in the country.

Teaching about the contributions of AfroChileans will lead to an increase in black pride. It will give them a platform in a country that has long made them invisible. Having a school curriculum about AfroChilean history will certainly go a long way in giving the Afro community more recognition. It will have the country acknowledge that Afro-Chileans are as much a part of the country as other Chilean citizens. It will hopefully help them assimilate into the country.

Paraguay

Paraguay is a nation whose Afro population has been invisible for most of its history. A recent law passed, 6940 Law, in Paraguay is designed for Afro-Paraguayans to be recognized in the country as well as to prevent forms of discrimination against them (UNSDG 2022). The fact that their contributions and existence are not known to most Paraguayans shows the racism of the country.

As photographer Mayeli Villalba (2021) says, many people of African descent struggle with their identity and how her aunt denied her African roots. Denying one's African roots will inevitably lead to the erasure and invisibility of a people, which is why Paraguay's Afro population is trying to be made visible. There is a small number of Afro-Paraguayans in the country. Some of the Afro-Paraguayans are two sub-tribes of Kenya's Kamba community, Kamba Cua and Kamba Kokue (Parker Diakite 2021). They descend from some of the first slaves brought to the country during

Spanish colonial rule (Diakite 2021). They have maintained their culture and identity despite attempts to erase it. They use their dances and cultural practices to bring to light their struggles (Diakite 2021).

The strides made in the country will hopefully allow Afro-Paraguayans to be assimilated into the country and be given equal opportunities. The country should focus on setting up quotas to enable the AfroParaguayan population to have more representation in workplaces. The recent law that was passed gives hope that the conditions of Afro-Paraguayans will improve.

There are still many challenges, however, to abolishing racial discrimination in Paraguay (UNSDG 2022). There needs to be more education about the history of Afro-Paraguayans. Racism in Paraguay should be treated as a serious matter. Increasing the visibility of Afro-Paraguayans will help in addressing the issues and challenges they face. The country should seek to uphold their legal rights and protections as well as help maintain their culture and identity.

The new law, 6940 Law, is supposed to help AfroParaguayans sustain inclusion in public policies at the country level (UNSDG 2022). We have to see how this law will play out in the years to come. It would help if they had elected officials who are Paraguayan, as well as giving them more representation in the private sector and government jobs.

Uruguay

Uruguay is a nation that has not been inclusive to those of African descent. Afro-Uruguayans experience racism in different forms. Afro-Uruguayans earn 11% less than the rest of Uruguayans while having a poverty rate of 20%, which is twice the country's rate (AFP 2020). While the country may claim to be inclusive and not racist, the reality is different. The fact that being black has a negative connotation is why many believe Afro-Uruguayans are underrepresented in the national statistics, according to the head of the Department of Afro-Descendants at the Ministry for Social Development, Amanda Diaz (AFP 2020).

There is the idea that denying one's African roots will make it easier to fit into Uruguayan society. According to the 2011 census, which was Uruguay's first census to include race, only 8% of Uruguay's population is of African descent (Eilis O'Neill 2013). Some argue that this number may be skewed due to the way the question on race was formulated and that the actual percentage may be up to twelve (O'Neill 2013). The fact that they first included race in the census goes to show how the country tries to hide any race problems.

Uruguay tries to not acknowledge racial issues due to the fact that they have created a myth of homogeneity (Parker Diakite 2021). This is despite the fact that there are racist chants heard at soccer matches. In 2013, officials in Uruguay were considering canceling soccer games if fans used racist chants during soccer matches (Manuel Rueda 2013).

Deborah Rodriguez, a track star in Uruguay, says she has been subjected to racial slurs all of her life (AFP 2020). Being that people of African descent are openly called slurs, even when they are famous athletes, shows that the country's claim of equality is a myth. They are not accepted in Uruguayan society, as are those who consider themselves of European descent. There was also an online campaign in Uruguay in 2013 to eliminate a racist expression from the Spanish language (Rueda 2013). The expression they sought to remove was "trabajar como un negro," which translates to "working like a black person" and harks back to the days when slaves would be overworked by their white masters (Rueda 2013).

Uruguay still has a way to go in order to create recognition for Afro-Uruguayans. At one point, it looked like Afro-Uruguayans would be able to achieve recognition and acknowledgment. The Black Native Party was created in 1936 in order to address the issues facing Afro-Uruguayans, but the party eventually dissolved, and there has yet to be another pro-black political party in Uruguay (Diakite 2021). Other movements have developed in recent years for AfroUruguayans to gain recognition.

In 2012, former president Jose Mujica promoted a quota program for Afro-Uruguayans and changed the law to incentivize companies that hire AfroUruguayans (Telesur 2015). This will give AfroUruguayans a larger presence in the workforce and presumably make them more visible to the public. This law will also mandate teaching the history of AfroUruguayans in schools (Amsterdam News 2012).

There is the "National Day of Candombe, AfroUruguayan Culture, and Racial Equality," which was established by law in 2006 to celebrate and create awareness of the impact African culture has had in Uruguay (Amsterdam News 2012). It is unfortunate they have had their history and existence erased in Uruguay to the point where these types of events are needed for Afro-Uruguayans to receive recognition of their existence. That is why activists work hard to fight for Afro-Uruguayans.

Activist Elizabeth Suarez talks about how African slaves formed the economic basis of Uruguay and were never given reparations (O'Neill 2013). The dictatorship in Uruguay from 1973 to 1985 also dealt a blow to AfroUruguayans due to the fact that many AfroUruguayans were uprooted from their homes and separated from the culture and community they had constructed (O'Neill 2013). This type of event would obviously create more hardships for Afro-Uruguayans.

This is why the government creating laws to help them is a big step in the right direction.

Afro-Uruguayans need to be socially included in Uruguayan society. Not doing so can have consequences for Uruguayan society as a whole. The people of Uruguay should be taught the history of Afro-Uruguayans as well as the contributions made by Afro-Uruguayans. This will give Afro-Uruguayans visibility in a positive manner and thus make it easier for them to be included and have their rights protected. It will allow people to not see them in a stereotypical manner.

The country needs to confront the fact that the myth of equality they have in Uruguay is just that, a myth. There needs to be serious dialogue on how racism plays a role in Uruguayan society and it is something that has to be dealt with accordingly. Simply ignoring the problem will not make it go away. There should be an increase of Afro-Uruguayan representation in the workplace, both in the private sector and government positions. This would help reduce the wealth gap in the country and also allow more opportunities for Afro-Uruguayans.

The new laws may lead to more opportunities and may increase black pride, but that may not be enough. The government should consider creating quota systems to help increase opportunity and representation for Afro-Uruguayans. The creation of another pro-black organization can also go a long way towards achieving progress for Afro-Uruguayans. Founded in 1988, Mundo Afro is one such organization, which lobbied for a gathering of racial data in 1996 and 2006, where the census showed a level of racial inequality in Uruguay (George Reid Andrews 2011). Mundo Afro should help in the advancement of Afro-Uruguayans. Giving Afro-Uruguayans a voice will go a long way to combating racism.

The country should also stop seeing itself as a European country and should look at itself as one that is multi-ethnic. The idea of whiteness being popular in the country is another challenge the country has in combating racism. That is another reason that giving

Afro-Uruguayans a voice is important since they can tell their experiences and have society understand their struggle. It is important to show another side of the country rather than the ideal vision of Uruguay being a European nation.

Argentina

Argentina is a country that has erased the history of black people from their country. The fact that Argentinians have been erased is due to a number of reasons. Black men were lost in the many wars taking place in the 1800's taking place in Argentina, starting with the war for independence in 1810 (Historyville 2022). This led to a ratio imbalance of black men and black women, which facilitated the rise of interracial marriages (Historyville 2022). This imbalance also led to black women having to choose either marrying Argentinian men or contesting for the few African men still around (Historyville 2022).

There are also other allegations made against the Argentinian government for the erasure of black people in Argentina. One such allegation is the one made about Domingo Faustino Sarmiento, who was president of Argentina from 1868 to 1874. He allegedly created repressive policies to wipe out black people, including the forced recruitment of black people into the army and forcing black people to remain in neighborhoods where disease would kill them off due to a lack of proper healthcare (Henry Louis Gates Jr. 2014).

These methods were used as a genocide against Afro-Argentinians. These were deliberate attempts to erase their history and presence altogether from Argentinian history. That is also why there were attempts to whiten Argentina through immigration from Europe, mainly from Spain and Italy (Gates Jr. 2014). By 1895, the number of Afro-Argentinians was so low that the government did not bother to include them in the national census (Gates Jr. 2014).

All of these policies led to the decline and almost complete disappearance of people of African descent in Argentina. Inevitably, anyone who is of African descent would experience discrimination in a nation that wants to be white and wants to whitewash their history and culture. In order for Afro-Argentinians to have a better shot at moving up the social ladder, they felt compelled to mix with Europeans in order to face less discrimination. Of course, race mixing to become lighter meant that they would lose their black identity not just in skin color and makeup but also in consciousness (Historyville 2022).

Today in Argentina, 90% of the population identifies as white, but many are unaware of their ancestry and do not truly know whether they have African ancestry or not (Historyville 2022). There have been some strides made in recent years to recognize the contributions made by Afro-Argentinians in the history and culture of Argentina despite many still in denial about Afro-Argentinians' influence in the country.

The candombe, which shares its origins with Uruguay, has the origins of the tango (Gates Jr. 2014). As for the tango, it is Argentina's cultural gift to the world and has African influence (Gates Jr. 2014). Though the country has tried to completely erase African influence and people from its history, black people have left their mark on the country.

There are some who will try to deny black history

in Argentina. In a 1998 article in The Montreal Gazette, a director at Buenos Aires Museum did not believe an Afro-Argentine exhibit should be put on display due to his belief that Afro-Argentine history is irrelevant to the country's history (Gates Jr. 2014). In that same article, when Argentina was set to play either Brazil or Nigeria in the Olympic finals, a newspaper had a headline reading "Bring on the monkeys" (Gates Jr. 2014).

Groups such as Africa Vive have been created to make people aware of Afro-Argentine history. One accomplishment they had was having the government allow the country to have a ceremony in 2001 to honor the country's black military heroes (Gates Jr. 2014). It is tragic that it has taken so long to get the country to acknowledge its black military heroes. Furthermore, in 2013, the day of November 3rd was assigned by the Argentine legislation as the day to celebrate Maria Remedios Del Valle, the Afro-Argentinian who fought in the war for Argentina's independence in the 1810's (Historyville 2022).

As hard as the country has tried to hide its

African influence, the truth is now slowly coming to light. These are just the first steps to what AfroArgentinians hope will lead to the country truly recognizing their history. Maybe Argentina will one day embrace its African roots. There needs to be a curriculum for AfroArgentinian history to be taught in Argentinian schools.

The country needs to become aware of the contributions and impact made to the culture and history of Argentina. This will also allow the rest of the world to learn about Afro-Argentinian influence in Argentina. Giving Afro-Argentinians a voice will help them progress and allow for their inclusion in Argentinian society.

The country should look to be accepting of people of African descent and acknowledge that many Argentinians have some black ancestry. Systemic racism needs to be addressed to allow opportunities for Afro-Argentinians to be represented in the workplace. Race and poverty go hand in hand in Argentina, as the ghettos in the country are full of

AfroArgentinians, as well as the country's prisons (Uki Goni 2021). They should be given more visibility in order for their presence in the country to be normalized. They need to show the world that there are people of African descent in the country.

The country should set up quotas and establish laws that protect the rights of Afro-Argentinians. Programs need to be created in order to help uplift Afro-Argentinians from poverty. There needs to be an attitude change in Argentina in regard to race and racism. They should be inclusive of Afro-Argentinians and acknowledge them as being full citizens of Argentina. A black identity should be normalized in Argentina. They should acknowledge that a large portion of the population in Argentina has black ancestry.

Venezuela

Venezuela is a nation where the contributions of Afro-Venezuelans are starting to get attention. May 10th is the Day of AfroVenezuelans, which honors the social, political, economic, and cultural contributions of AfroVenezuelans (Amara Amaryah 2022). There have been initiatives created to raise awareness of the contributions made by Afro-Venezuelans.

In 2005, then-president Hugo Chavez launched an initiative to create this type of awareness and to educate people on Afro-Venezuelan contributions (Amaryah 2022). Chavez also passed anti-discrimination laws to combat racism in Venezuela (Amaryah 2022). These changes have been necessary for Afro-Venezuelans to progress and acknowledge their contributions.

Historians of the Annales School have argued that slavery left a socioeconomic hierarchy based on skin color and race (Menika Dirkson 2022). Race and socioeconomic status go hand in hand in Venezuela. The policies enacted to fight systemic racism were just the beginning of what is needed to fight racial inequality.

As scholar Winthrop Wright concluded in his investigation into racism, that opportunities for AfroVenezuelans to move up the socioeconomic ladder have been limited due to racial stereotypes, colorism, immigration bans on black foreigners, and political propaganda on whitening the country (Dirkson 2022). Venezuela is a country that has tried to make amends for its legacy of slavery though some methods have received backlash for the way it has tried to do so. The methods used by Hugo Chavez, who sought to narrow the racial discrimination gap by taking land and money from the wealthy to provide food, healthcare, and education for the poor, infuriated affluent Venezuelans (Dirkson 2022).

Afro-Venezuelans and the poor were those who were predominantly "Chavista," those who were in favor of Chavez (Dirkson 2022). It appears that Chavez had support from Afro-Venezuelans who not only wanted recognition for their contributions to Venezuela but also who wanted to not experience racial discrimination. Despite all of the efforts made by Chavez, there is still overt racism in Venezuela.

Sociologist Zulima Paredes says that everything that comes from being black is seen as bad (AFP 2021). This is why hair discrimination is common in Venezuela. Afro-Venezuelans are taught in school that you cannot enter school with an Afro hairstyle, thus indoctrinating them at a very young age (AFP 2021). This type of attitude will obviously lead to Afro-Venezuelans having low self-esteem and denying their black identity.

The country has a complicated relationship with its cultural identity despite a law passed in 2011 that bans racial discrimination (AFP 2021). The fact that Venezuela sees Afro hair and everything related to blackness as bad may explain why the country shows the world the models that it does at beauty pageants. Venezuela has won the Miss Universe title seven times, and all seven times, the winning contestant was a fairskinned woman with straight or straightened hair, which shows the country's beauty standard is that of a Western European type (AFP 2021).

The country's perception of this type of beauty will lead to discrimination against Afro-Venezuelan women who would do well in representing the country in beauty pageants. It also leads to discrimination in other aspects of society. According to Sarai Coscojuela (2021), an Afro-Venezuelan woman named Eileyn Ugueto experienced discrimination as a young girl in school and even within her own family. The fact that people will see their own relatives in a negative way due to having African features shows how racism is entrenched in Venezuela.

Venezuela should open itself up to where hair is not an issue in whether or not someone obtains a job or is considered presentable. The country needs to confront its racism. The Venezuelan government denies racism and portrays itself as a racial democracy that embraces its coffee-with-milk characteristic with pride (Muzamil Fatima 2021). The notion of racism has been masked by the ideology of mestizaje by categorizing everyone as mixed (Fatima 2021).

Denying racism will only create more grievance for those who suffer from it. It is tragic how the country has erased the contributions of Afro-Venezuelans. That is why the policies passed by Chavez were important for Afro-Venezuelans. It was a hope created to open doors for them.

As it currently stands, Afro-Venezuelans lack proper representation in the media, workforce, and are denied documents such as birth certificates, information on social security issues, and nationality (Fatima 2021). All this leads to Afro-Venezuelans being excluded from society. They are not seen as the norm and are often perceived as being less than fair-skinned Venezuelans.

One issue in Venezuela is that there is a double standard where there is a discourse of inclusion, yet there are fewer opportunities for Afro-Venezuelans (Cira Pascual Marquina 2021). This double standard makes it harder to address the issues involving racism.

There is the belief that anyone who speaks up about racism is living a fantasy (Marquina 2021). Giving AfroVenezuelans a voice will help address the issues of racism.

It is also important that the issues facing AfroVenezuelans do not get mixed up with issues facing other marginalized Venezuelans due to any coalition. There has been an attempt at homogenization and the erasure of black identity due to a nationalistic discourse that puts the national or mestizo culture above the problems faced by Afro-Venezuelans (Marquina 2021). Obviously, putting on a discourse for the nation as a whole would lead to overlooking issues facing AfroVenezuelans.

Any Afro-Venezuelan leaders or organizations need to focus strictly on issues facing Afro-Venezuelans. Having a discourse only on a broad class struggle will not resolve racism. The government should create quotas to have Afro-Venezuelans better represented in different job sectors. They should create TV programs to portray Afro-Venezuelans in a positive manner. The biggest challenge is to get people to admit there is racism in Venezuela. Until then, racism will continue to be an issue.

Dominican Republic

The Dominican Republic is a nation that has openly expressed anti-black sentiments against their own people. According to Manuel Barcia (2013), a study indicated that children between the ages of 4 and 13 would associate evil, ugliness, and poverty with black people rather than white people. The country also has wanted to get rid of people of Haitian descent.

Though the Dominican Constitution states that anyone born in the Dominican Republic is a Dominican citizen, this does not apply to those born while in transit (Barcia 2013). The meaning of *in transit* is open to interpretation, but it can have serious ramifications for a large portion of the population. In 2013, the Dominican Republic Constitutional Court ruled that those born in the country after 1929 should no longer be considered Dominican citizens if their parents were not Dominican, which would affect a quarter million Dominicans (Barcia 2013). This is part of the anti-

Haitian sentiment the Dominican Republic has expressed over the years.

It seems the country feels invaded by those of Haitian descent and feels a need to have them deported, even though they only speak Spanish and have Dominican customs. The court ruling would eventually leave more than 200,000 people of Haitian descent without a nationality, though some children and others were allowed to apply for citizenship in 2014 amid international pressure (Arturo Conde 2021).

According to documentary director Michele Stephenson, the island is the birth of the racial caste system across the Western hemisphere due to the fact that it is the place where the first Europeans and Africans arrived as well as where the first genocide took place and where the racial caste first manifested itself (Conde 2021). This fact shows why the Dominican Republic has racist attitudes towards anything related to African origins. The country has yet to move past the idea of associating black people with anything negative. This attitude will inevitably lead to Dominicans denying their blackness. There are also many in denial about racism in the country.

Former Dominican president Danilo Medina has stated that Dominicans cannot be racist, being that over 80% of the country is made up of blacks and mulattoes and that Haitians live and coexist everywhere with Dominicans in the country (Conde 2021). This type of denial will not resolve the racial issues in the country. A lot of people paint this as merely an issue between the Dominican Republic and Haiti, but you do not see any bad actions done by Haiti against Dominicans (Natasha Alford 2022).

Anti-blackness is so prevalent that even black Americans have to watch out when they travel to the Dominican Republic. The U.S. embassy has warned black Americans who travel down to the Dominican Republic to carry their passports with them, as there have been reports of Dominican immigration officials stopping people based on their skin color (Alford 2022). This type of news would not do well for a country that makes a lot of money off tourism.

It appears that the country does do what it can to whiten up its society. Dominicans are often taught that they are a white Spanish nation, while Haitians are an African Creole-speaking nation, thus giving Dominicans a feeling of racial superiority (Alford 2022). The country has a history of using violence to attempt to whiten itself.

In 1937, dictator Raphael Trujillo, who was an admirer of Hitler and secretly had Haitian ancestry himself, ordered the massacre of about 20,000 Haitians (Alford 2022). This was an obvious genocide that continues to this day in a different fashion. The Dominican Republic is not treating Venezuelan immigrants who overstay their visas in this manner and is also offering help to Ukrainian refugees (Alford 2022). All these facts remove any doubt as to what the real reason Haitians are being deported from the Dominican Republic.

In order to overcome anti-black racism in the Dominican Republic, they should start by teaching the real history of the country. They should teach people about the contributions made by Afro-Dominicans. They should remove the negativity associated with blackness. The country needs to acknowledge the problem they have with racism in order to resolve it. The country should acknowledge the Haitian roots many Dominicans have and not look down on Haitians. The Dominican Republic should not look to the idea of trying to lighten up the nation by having people from other countries migrate to the country while Haitians of Dominican descent are being deported.

The court ruling to deport Dominicans of Haitian descent born after 1929 if their parents were not Dominicans is a very racist ruling that should be overturned. It unfairly targets those Dominicans of Haitian descent. It is an attempt to remove people they see as undesirable due to skin color. The Dominican Republic should acknowledge the African influence in their society and culture. They need to be taught that they have African ancestry and to embrace their African heritage. They should acknowledge that many of them have Haitian blood and to be acceptable to those of

Haitian descent.

It is wrong for such xenophobia to exist in the Dominican Republic. They should seek to promote more positive images of black people on TV in order to not view blackness in a negative manner.

Cuba

In Cuba, anti-black racism permeates society. Though the government claims that the Communist revolution eliminated racism, it is very much alive on the island. The irony to all this is the fact Cuba criticizes the United States for their systemic racism. In 1960, Fidel Castro traveled to New York City for a United Nations meeting, where he stayed at the Hotel Theresa in Harlem, met with Malcolm X, and made it clear he stood with African Americans in their fight for racial equality (Rebecca Bodenheimer 2020).

Cuba has also granted political asylum to black nationalists and members of the Black Panther Party wanted by the FBI (Bodenheimer 2020). Despite these actions, the Cuban government has failed to acknowledge racism within its own borders. Cuba's race problems have been obscured by the fact that they have a notion that the country cannot have racism when they have such a large mixed-race population, along with the country's views on race being reducible to class (Bodenheimer 2020).

The fact that Castro prohibited any discourse on racism also did not help. Anyone who spoke out against racism in Cuba was branded a "counterrevolutionary" and therefore faced punishment or had to seek exile in another country (Bodenheimer 2020). The fact that Cuba is not willing to look into racism in their society obviously means that racial inequalities will not be resolved.

It is rather hypocritical for Cuba to criticize the United States on racism, especially when it comes to social justice, while at the same time not addressing those same issues in their country. In 2020, Cuban news stations provided extensive coverage of the killing of George Floyd at the hands of Minneapolis police officers but, at the same time, were rather quiet on similar incidents involving Afro-Cubans (Bodenheimer 2020).

In Cuba, Afro-Cubans are often racially profiled by police. There are also cases where Black Americans may be mistaken to be Afro-Cuban by police and therefore be subjected to being stopped and harassed by police (Bodenheimer 2020). The police will detain and ask for identification of young Afro-Cuban men more frequently than non-black Cubans, especially if they are walking with a white foreigner, in an attempt to do what they believe needs to be done to protect white tourists (Bodenheimer 2020).

Anti-black racism in Cuba runs deep. While the country looks to project an image to the outside world that racism no longer exists on the island, the reality is much different. The denial of race in Cuban society and acting colorblind is hindering any action to do away with systemic racism on the island. Scholar Tomas Fernandez Robaina says that knowing the history of Afro-Cubans is important for all Cubans, and teaching Afro-Cuban history in schools can awaken the youth (B. Denise Hawkins 2017).

Acknowledging the Afro-Cuban struggle and learning about their accomplishments can obviously change the perception of Afro-Cubans on the island. The country has persuaded itself with the idea of mestizaje, which is a racial mix, as a way to establish Cuban national identity (Bodenheimer 2020). This idea will mean that those who do not fit this description will not have the same privileges as those who are seen as mixed. This is probably why, on the national census, there is a suspiciously low number of people identifying as black.

In the 2012 census, just 9.3% identified as black, while 64.3% identified as white (Hawkins 2017). There are scholars who put the percentage of Afro-Cubans as being between 33% and 60%, while the United States government puts it at 75% (Hawkins 2017). These contradictory figures may indicate that Afro-Cubans try to blend into society by not seeing themselves as black but rather just as mixed. They may not want to be associated with being black due to the negative stereotypes and how blacks are not seen in a good light. The country needs to focus on addressing its issues of racism in order to create a more just society. They need to have the police not stereotype AfroCuban men and treat them as if they are potentially doing something wrong.

In Cuba, there is a much-needed dialogue on racism. The government should loosen restrictions on speech about racism in order to not only acknowledge racism but also find ways to address it. The country should find a way to create more economic opportunities for Afro-Cubans. They should have the Afro-Cuban community better represented in job sectors, particularly those in the tourist industry.

Cuba should promote the teaching of AfroCuban history and promote the idea of people embracing their African roots. This would enable AfroCubans to identify as black on a national census and also give them a voice so they can address the issues facing them.

The country should allow for the formation of black political parties to create progress for AfroCubans. The fact that Cuba has looked to suppress any discussions on racism while at the same time criticizing the United States is very hypocritical and is also a way to deflect from its own issues with racism.

The country should allow for festivities displaying Afro-Cuban culture so the people in Cuba can learn about AfroCuban culture as well as help blend Afro-Cubans into Cuban society. It will help expose the rest of the country to what being Afro-Cubans is all about and could lead to more opportunities for Afro-Cubans in the tourism industry. It could also help reduce stereotypical views of Afro-Cubans.

The only way Cuba will end racism is by confronting it. Making it a taboo or "counterrevolutionary" topic will only help maintain the status quo and thus have a racially unequal nation.

Puerto Rico

In Puerto Rico, there is a denial of anti-black racism. There is a notion that everyone in Puerto Rico is mixed, which makes black people invisible while at the same time upholding those who are fair-skinned as being the norm and a universal social category (Hilda Llorens 2020). This leads to black people in Puerto Rico being unable to address anti-black racism on the island. In Puerto Rico, they see someone black as being from other islands, such as Haiti, the Dominican Republic, or Cuba (Grace Asiegbu 2020). The U.S. census gives Puerto Ricans fewer racial options than what is commonly used on the island, and the racial spectrum used their works in a binary, such as how black one looks very how white one looks (Llorens 2020). The fact that being black is seen as foreign can also lead to a denial of black identity and, through this invisibility, make it harder to address racial inequalities on the island.

In a 2017 survey, among those who identified as

"black," 71% reported experiencing racism, and the study showed that the darker the person, the more likely they were to report experiencing racism (Llorens 2020). Afro-Puerto Ricans are more likely to live in areas with serious environmental pollution, such as Vieques and Guayama, or live in areas with fewer resources and are vulnerable to gentrification and the impacts of climate change, like in Loiza (Asiegbu 2020).

In Puerto Rico, people who are of darker skin are referred to as "trigueño" rather than black so as to not be seen as a foreigner (Asiegbu 2020). The idea that Puerto Rican identity is associated with being of mixed race creates an identity issue for people on the island. The problem is that there is a negative connotation associated with identifying as black, and therefore identifying as white has its privileges (Asiegbu 2020).

Puerto Rican nationalism has been used to exclude Afro-Puerto Ricans (Llorens 2020). It is obviously very challenging to combat systemic inequalities with the denial of race and racism and simultaneously denying the existence or identity of black people in Puerto Rico. It creates a divide that the island is not willing to confront. It can erase the contributions of black people in Puerto Rico.

There are movements to teach people about the contributions of Afro-Puerto Ricans to increase a black identity on the island. Colectivo Ile, a coalition of Puerto Rican educators and organizers, holds educational workshops across Puerto Rico, teaching about the contributions of Afro-Puerto Ricans and teach about African civilizations, all in an attempt to get more people to identify as black on the census (Natasha S. Alford 2020).

It is important to emphasize the contributions of Afro-Puerto Ricans in order to create black pride on the island. People are ashamed to be associated with blackness. There is a feeling that it will erase their Puerto Rican nationalism. There are people who believe using the term "black" is an insult, and they have the idea of "mejorar la raza," which means "bettering the race," an idea that is common throughout Latin America, where fair skin is seen as superior to dark skin

(Alford 2020) . Maybe efforts taken by activists and educators will start to change people's views on blackness in Puerto Rico.

They should show positive images on TV of black people in order to make people more educated and not resort to stereotypes. The island has to change its perception of blacks as being foreign and acknowledge that there are people of African descent who are just as Puerto Rican as those who are fair-skinned. Teaching people about the influence and contributions made by Afro-Puerto Ricans will lead to more acceptance of a black identity in Puerto Rico and also make more people identify as black. It will increase racial pride for those who identify as black.

Having a dialogue on racism in Puerto Rico is important in order to address racism. Simply being in denial of racism will only hinder any progress towards eliminating racism. It appears the biggest obstacle to addressing racism in Puerto Rico is acknowledging the existence of a black identity and heritage on the island. Having a quota system may do a lot to combat racial discrimination in the workplace and admissions for universities if people refuse to acknowledge their black heritage.

The people on the island should allow for AfroPuerto Ricans to blend into the society on the island. Afro-Puerto Ricans should be acknowledged as being part of the island. They need to also do away with any negative association of blackness on the island. The people in Puerto Rico should realize while they are all Puerto Ricans, Afro-Puerto Ricans have their unique issues, and simply identifying by national origin means that it will prevent systemic inequalities from being addressed. Their ethnicity should be recognized in order to address the systemic racism on the island.

Brazil

Brazil is a country where there is a denial of the existence of systemic racism. Throughout the 20th century, the elites in Brazil have promoted the idea that the country is a "racial democracy," where the mix of European, African, and Indigenous cultures have mixed harmoniously (Ciara Nugent and Thais Regina 2020). There is a belief that there cannot be racism or racial conflict due to the mix in the country. Though the idea of a mixture is promoted, the truth is that there has been an encouragement of "lightening up" the country.

Politicians, the media, and academics have all encouraged Afro-Brazilians to marry and have children with fair-skinned Brazilians and with European immigrants to have light-skinned children (Nugent and Regina, 2020). The country has become aware of racism in recent years, especially with them witnessing Black Lives Matter protests in the United States.

In 2012, the Brazilian Supreme Court recognized

the legality of racial quotas in public universities for Afro-Brazilians (Raphael Tsavkko Garcia 2020). The fact that fair-skinned Brazilians deny the existence of antiblack racism in the country is rather ironic, being that Afro-Brazilians disproportionately suffer from police brutality, less education, higher unemployment rates, less representation in prominent positions of power, and higher rates of murder (Tsavkko Garcia 2020).

During the COVID-19 pandemic, Afro-Brazilians had higher death rates and lost their jobs at higher rates as well (Nugent and Regina, 2020). In 2019, President Jair Bolsonaro pushed a bill that allows police to use blanket "self-defense" in the use of deadly force (Nugent and Regina 2020). The country obviously does not care about people of African descent in the country. The fact that they are in denial will make it harder to combat racism though an increase in racial awareness in recent years is a step in the right direction. Brazil has a long way to go, especially with the Bolsonaro administration having far-right ideologies that look to suppress any movements toward achieving equality.

One way in which Afro-Brazilians are looking to bring awareness of anti-black racism and embrace their black identity is through the formation of *quilombos*, which is basically the creation of a space for AfroBrazilians to address issues affecting them in the country (Nugent and Regina 2020). This is a way for them to create spaces to resolve the issues they have. It will also lead to a rise in embracing their African roots and expressing pride in their African heritage. In fact, the embrace of a black identity is already taking place. According to Afro-Brazilian writer and activist Bianca Santana, mixed-race people in Brazil are increasingly identifying as black and embracing their black identity (AFP 2021). One reason for that could be quotas being introduced for college admissions and in hiring for government jobs. Identifying as black nowadays is seen as valuable in Brazil due to the quotas and is seen as fundamental to having self-knowledge (AFP 2021).

Having quotas in universities and the workplace will increase the number of Afro-Brazilians in those positions and will give hope to Afro-Brazilians who have felt excluded from many parts of Brazilian society. It can help reduce the stigma of identifying as black in the country. The goal for many in Brazil was to identify as white because being black was seen as bad (AFP 2021). Now, there is less of a need to do this. It will only help increase the recognition and accomplishments of Afro-Brazilians. Doing this will help give rise to black pride and identity in the country.

Giving Afro-Brazilians a voice will help them address issues facing their community. The creation of quotas is definitely a big step towards reducing systemic racism and increasing visibility for Afro-Brazilians. There needs to be a dialogue on addressing the racism in the country. Suppressing any discussions will only help maintain the status quo and thus prevent Afro-Brazilians from achieving equality. They should create programs on TV that portray Afro-Brazilians in a positive light and thus make people more sympathetic to their cause.

The criminal justice system could use reform,

being that Afro-Brazilians experience police brutality at higher rates. Brazil needs to stop living in denial of its racism and actively look to combat racism. Afro-Brazilians should be allowed to blend into Brazilian society rather than be ostracized and denied basic resources.

Having people acknowledge their African ancestry is definitely one way to have the issues facing Afro-Brazilians addressed. It will also help enforce laws that prohibit racial discrimination. They should also not have people see dark skin as being negative while glorifying light skin. There needs to be an attitude change on how people see blackness in the country.

Teaching people about the contributions of Afro-Brazilians and how it has influenced their culture can help address racism as well as get people to not look down on Afro-Brazilians. In Brazil, there are many challenges to achieving a racially equal society.

Some steps have been taken to attempt to address the issues, but there is still more work to be done.

Conclusion

As we have seen, there is a denial of racism in many Latin American countries, while others tried to deny the existence of people of African descent in their countries. Racism is a major issue in Latin America. While it has become easier for many to simply deny a black identity or make a claim that in a racially mixed society, there can be no racism, the fact is that simply ignoring a problem or pretending it does not exist will not make the problem go away.

Racism is a major issue when it involves the livelihood of people of African descent, whether it's politically, socially, and/or economically. People of African descent may be treated as foreigners in their birth countries due to a lack of acceptance from the rest of society in those particular countries. It is important that they be given a voice in order to no longer have their issues overlooked and to have visibility as a people and culture.

Latin countries need to realize that poverty is

not just a class issue but also an issue where skin color and socioeconomic status go hand in hand. Latin countries need to be accepting of people of African descent and have them blend into their societies. The dominant societies should be taught about the history of black people in Latin America and should have Afro-descendants be given a better image through the media. They should increase awareness of how people of African descent are simply looking to accomplish the same things that other people in those societies are trying to accomplish. It is just as important that any movements by activists should not be co-opted. The societies in Latin countries should understand people of African descent have unique challenges and issues to address. There should be a focus specifically on helping people of African descent in Latin countries.

Article Index

<u>MEXICO</u>

- Racism in Mexico | Black Women Abroad (youtube.com)

- 'We exist. We're here': Afro-Mexicans make the census after long struggle for recognition | Mexico | The Guardian

- Mexico 2020's Census: Results Show Afro-Mexican Identity (remezcla.com)

HONDURAS

- Race and racism in Honduran soccer and society - The Washington Post

- People of African descent in Honduras: Advocating for justice and inspiring change | OHCHR

- Persecuted Afro-Hondurans push for state protection | Human Rights News | Al Jazeera

- Afro-Indigenous People in Honduras Are Being Forcibly Displaced. Washington Is Complicit. - In These Times

- The Garifuna in Honduras: A History of Pillage and Dispossession — Hampton Institute (hamptonthink.org)

- Who are the Garifuna People? - Honduras Travel

GUATEMALA

- The Garífuna Voices of Guatemala's Armed Conflict | NACLA

- Black Caribs honor endangered culture in Guatemala | Reuters

- Garífuna Voices of Guatemala: Central America's Overlooked Segment of the African Diaspora – COHA

- Everything You Need To Know About The History Of Afro-Guatemalans - Travel Noire

- Livingston, Where Garifuna Culture In Guatemala Still Exists Today - Travel Noire

EL SALVADOR

- El Salvador and its history of Black exclusion | Amandala Newspaper

- COMMITTEE ON ELIMINATION OF RACIAL DIS-CRIMINATION CONSIDERS REPORT OF EL SAL-VADOR | OHCHR

NICARAGUA

- How Young Afro Nicaraguan People Are Fighting To Be Heard and Seen - Travel Noire

- Why My Nicaraguan Father Did Not "See" His Blackness - Havana Times

- How Afro-Nicaraguans Suffer Through the 'Taboo' Subject of Racism (atlantablackstar.com)

- Nicaragua at a Revolutionary Crossroads and in Imperialist Crosshairs | Un enfoque diferente - Nicaragua - a different focus (tortillaconsal.com)

- I Witnessed the Truth about Nicaragua - Hood Communist

COSTA RICA

- The White Myth - The roots of racial discrimination and the myth of racial homogeneity in Costa Rica - DEBAT (debatmagazine.nl)

- Inside Límon: The Land Of Afro-Costa Ricans - Travel Noire

- The intricate history of black Costa Ricans, who were only recognised as citizens in 1949 - Face2Face Africa

- Afro-Costa Rican's History of Inequality & Long Road to Pura Vida (theclick.news)

- Democracy and Ethnic Conflict: Blacks in Costa Rica | Q COSTA RICA

- Costa Rica Just Elected Its First Black Female Vice President - Okayplayer (okayafrica.com)

- Costa Rica is an Afro-descendants country – The Expat Database

PANAMA

- Afro-Panamanians Preserve their Cultural Identity | Latina Republic

- In Panama, a Youth Soccer Group Leads the Charge Against Racism & Economic Impacts of COVID-19 - Okayplayer (okayafrica.com)

- Inside Isla Cólon: The Land Of Afro-Panamani-ans - Travel Noire

COLOMBIA

- Reclaiming Colombia's Black history, one tour at a time | The World from PRX

- What It Means To Be Black In Colombia - Travel Noire

- Colombia While Black:Double-Consciousness Abroad (ebony.com)

- Colombia's first Black vice president Francia Marquez vows to reduce inequality (nbcnews.com)

- Afro-Colombian Leaders: Recognition of Race and the Struggle to Realize Change - Americas Quarterly

- Yes, Racism is Alive in Colombia – MCC LACA

- The Black Lives Matter Movement Is Resonating in Colombia (vice.com)

<u>ECUADOR</u>

- Ecuador: Discrimination and environmental racism against people of African descent must end, say UN experts | OHCHR

- Blackness and Beauty in Ecuador | ReVista (harvard.edu)

- 'Not Nannies or Cooks': Afro-Ecuadorean Women Fight Back | News | teleSUR English

<u>PERU</u>

- Peru's minorities battle racism - BBC News

- Black and Invisible in Peru | ReVista (harvard.edu)

<u>BOLIVIA</u>

- Bolivia's little-known tribal kingdom (bbc.com)

- The Afro-Bolivians And Their Monarchy In Bolivia: An Enigmatic Kingdom | Ancient Origins (ancient-origins.net)

- Bolivian Express | A New Era for the Afro-Bolivian?

CHILE

- The History and Historiography of Afro-Chileans in Colonial Chile (epoch-magazine.com)

- Recognizing Blackness in Chile – Guernica (guernicamag.com)

- How Afro-Chileans Are Fighting To Be Recognized In Chile - Travel Noire

- Interview: How Black Feminists in Chile are Challenging The Country's Whitewashed Identity - Okayplayer (okayafrica.com)

- Afro-Chileans Finally Recognized as Culture in Chile - Chile Today

URUGUAY

- Study: Blacks in Uruguay still suffering under systemic racism (trtworld.com)

- Afro-Uruguay: A Brief History • (blackpast.org)

- Curbing discrimination – DW – 11/15/2013

- Black Native Party: The Political Party That Once Gave Afro-Uruguayan People Hope - Travel Noire

- Afro-Urugayan law sets path to affirmative action - New York Amsterdam News

- Petition Asks Linguists to Remove Racist Expressions from Spanish Dictionary - ABC News (go.com)

- Uruguay Committed to Recognizing African Descendants | News | teleSUR English

PARAGUAY

- UNSDG | UN team supports Paraguay in combatting discrimination against people of African descent

- Being black in Paraguay - Vist Projects

- Kamba Cua: The Little Known Kenyan Tribe Living In South America For 200 Years - Travel Noire

<u>ARGENTINA</u>

- Afro-Argentines: How Argentina Erased Its Black People From History – HistoryVille (thehistoryville.com)

- True or False: There Are No Black People in Argentina (theroot.com)

- Time to challenge Argentina's white European self-image, black history experts say | Argentina | The Guardian

<u>VENEZUELA</u>

- La Afrovenezolanidad: A Historiography of the Black Experience in Venezuela - AAIHS

- The Afro-Venezuelan Culture And History That Is Being Celebrated And Protected - Travel Noire

- Embracing the Afro in revolt against Venezuela's 'bad hair' stereotype - France 24

- Beauty stereotypes in Venezuela tainted by racism - La Prensa Latina Media

- You could have been black too: Describing racism in Venezuela - Modern Diplomacy

- Afro-Venezuelan Culture and Resistance: A Conversation with Ines Perez-Wilke - Venezuelanalysis

DOMINICAN REPUBLIC

- Why is the Dominican Republic deporting Black people to Haiti? Activists say it's history repeating itself (yahoo.com)

- Dominican Republic's enduring history of racism against Haitians explored in 'Stateless' (nbcnews.com)

- Xenophobia and racism back in the Dominican Republic | Opinions | Al Jazeera

CUBA

- Cuba Loves to Criticize the United States, but the Island Has Its Own Police Racism Problem (foreignpolicy.com)

- In Cuba, African Roots Run Deep, but It's a Lesson Students Aren't Learning in the Classroom (nbcnews.com)

<u>PUERTO RICO</u>

- 'Racialization works differently here in Puerto Rico, do not bring your U.S.-centric ideas about race here!' - AAIHS

- Why Some Black Puerto Ricans Choose 'White' on the Census - The New York Times (nytimes.com)

- Blackness in Puerto Rico - Medill Reports Chicago (northwestern.edu)

<u>BRAZIL</u>

- How Black Brazilians Are Fighting Racial Injustice Today | TIME

- Diversity in Brazil is still just an illusion | Racism | Al Jazeera

- Mixed-race Brazilians increasingly embrace blackness (france24.com)